LET'S JUST READ NURSERY RHYMES AS THEY ARE.

MOSTLY BRITISH ONES, LARGELY BECAUSE THOSE ARE THE ONES THAT I REALLY KNOW, BUT A FEW FROM FAR AFIELD TOO.

HARD, AS WE RARELY KNOW THEIR ORIGINS.

KIDS SONGS IN THE LOCAL TONGUE JUST WEREN'T CONSIDERED IMPORTANT ENOUGH TO WRITE DOWN UNTIL THE LATE 18TH CENTURY.

DIFFERENT VERSIONS FROM AREA TO AREA ADD CONFUSION. THEN SOME WRITERS GOT CREATIVE, THEIR ALTERED VERSIONS REPLACING THE ORIGINALS.

NOW WEB AND TELEVISION ARE PUSHING EVEN MORE CHANGE. SOFTENING THEM UP, INJECTING NEW MORALS, OR EVEN CHANGING THEM COMPLETELY.

THIS MAY NOT BE A BAD THING. THEY WERE ALWAYS EVOLVING, BUT THIS BOOK TRIES TO REACH BACK AND LOOK AGAIN.

THESE RHYMES WERE RARELY SOFT AND, BY TODAY'S STANDARDS, NOT STRICTLY MORAL. THEY AND THEIR CREATORS ARE MUCH MORE, THEY'RE INTERESTING.

SO I INVITE YOU TO REVEL IN THEIR PLEASURES, WEEP FOR THEIR PAINS, REEL AT THEIR SAVAGERY, AND STARE AGAPE AT THEIR ODDITY.

ENJOY

TWINKLE TWINKLE LITTLE STAR
HOW I WONDER WHAT YOU ARE
UP ABOVE THE WORLD SO HIGH
LIKE A DIAMOND IN THE SKY
TWINKLE TWINKLE LITTLE STAR
HOW I WONDER WHAT YOU ARE

THIS RHYME WE KNOW ABOUT, AND
IT'S MELODY TOO.

CONTRARY TO POPULAR BELIEF MOZART
DIDN'T WRITE IT EITHER WHEN
HE WAS FIVE, OR AT ALL, FOR THAT
MATTER. THE TUNE FEATURES IN ONE
OF HIS SYMPHONIES, BUT IS A FRENCH
FOLK SONG CALLED "AH VOUS DIRAI-JE,
MAMAN".

THIS TUNE, WITH A BIT OF FLOURISH
IS ALSO THE TUNE TO BAH BAH BLACK
SHEEP.

THE WORDS WERE WRITTEN BY JANE
TAYLOR AND PUBLISHED IN 1806 IN A
BOOK OF SONGS BY HER SISTER ANNE.

THE FULL POEM HAS FIVE VERSES,
BUT MOST OF THE WORLD KNOWS ONLY
THE ONE.

LEWIS CARROL "HOMAGED" THIS RHYME
IN ALICE IN WONDERLAND, HENCE
THE BAT AND TEA TRAY PICTURED
HERE.SOMEBODY REALLY SHOULD
UPDATE THIS TO MATCH MODERN
SCIENCE.

"LIKE A FURNACE IN THE SKY"

RAIN RAIN
GO AWAY
COME AGAIN
ANOTHER DAY

THIS RHYME CAN BE DATED BACK
AS FAR AS THE SEVENTEENTH
CENTURY IN ENGLISH BUT OF
COURSE HAS SIMILAR VARIANTS
SPANNING THROUGH HISTORY AND
ACCROSS EUROPE, IF NOT THE
WORLD.

IN MY ADULTHOOD, I HAVE HEARD
THIS SUNG WITH ADDED VERSES,
AND SUNG TO A VARIANT OF THE
RING-A-RING OF ROSES MELODY.

TRADITIONALLY, THIS RHYME IS
MEANT NOT TO BE SUNG, BUT
CHANTED. IT IS A SPELL.
FROM MEMORY IT DOESNT WORK
BUT IT'S FUNNY TO SEE IT'S
SURVIVAL ALONGSIDE GOOSEY
GOOSEY GANDER. THE STRANGE
MAN PICTURED HERE HAS GOT IT
WORKING, AND EVEN THE LAKE
BEHIND IS SHYING AWAY.

GOOSEY GOOSEY GANDER
WHITHER DO YOU WANDER
UPSTAIRS DOWNSTAIRS
NIGHTLY IN THY CHAMBERS

THERE I SAW AN OLD MAN
WHO WOLUDN'T SAY HIS PRAYERS
SO I TOOK HIM BY HIS LEG
AND I THREW HIM DOWN THE
STAIRS

SOME BELIEVE THAT THE GOOSE
APPEARS AS A RELIC OF PAGAN
IDEOLOGIES, BUT GOOSEY GOOSEY
GANDER IS MOST LIKELY A CHARMING
TALE OF RELIGIOUS PERSECUTION.

THE OLD MAN NOT PRAYING EITHER
BECAUSE HE IS CATHOLIC OR BECAUSE
HE IS NOT.

EITHER WAY, HE IS IN BAD COMPANY,
AND THE "RIGHT WAY" IS BEING
FORCED UPON HIM WITH TOOTH AND
CLAW.A TRIP TO THE PARK WITH
A LOAF OF BREAD WILL QUICKLY
HIGHLIGHT GEESE AS A FORCE TO BE
RECKONED WITH, AND NOTABLY GEESE
MAKE EXCELLENT "GUARD DOGS".

IF GEESE GOT RELIGIOUS ON US, WE'D
BE IN TROUBLE.

BAD GOOSEY!

BAD BAD GOOSEY!

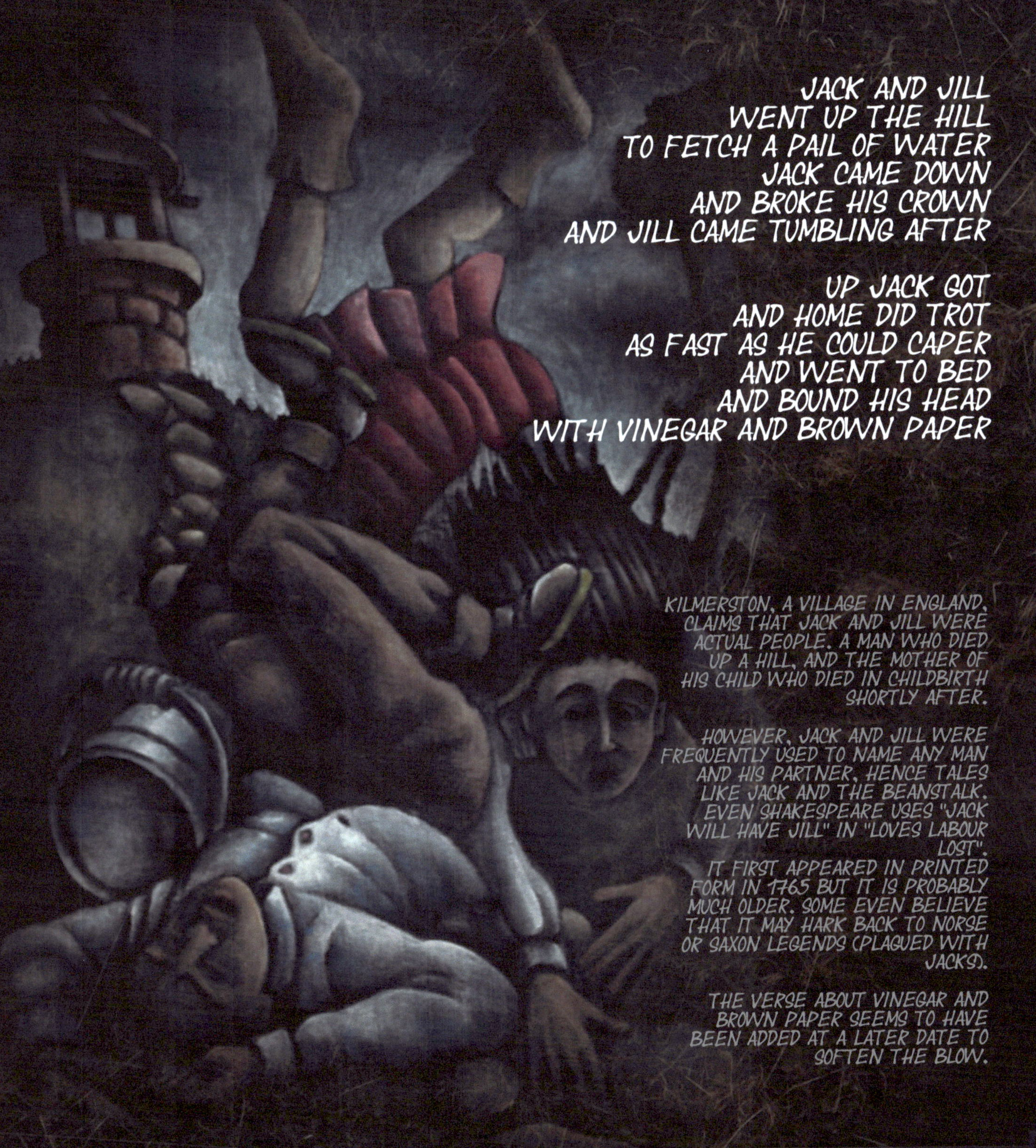

JACK AND JILL
WENT UP THE HILL
TO FETCH A PAIL OF WATER
JACK CAME DOWN
AND BROKE HIS CROWN
AND JILL CAME TUMBLING AFTER

UP JACK GOT
AND HOME DID TROT
AS FAST AS HE COULD CAPER
AND WENT TO BED
AND BOUND HIS HEAD
WITH VINEGAR AND BROWN PAPER

KILMERSTON, A VILLAGE IN ENGLAND,
CLAIMS THAT JACK AND JILL WERE
ACTUAL PEOPLE. A MAN WHO DIED
UP A HILL, AND THE MOTHER OF
HIS CHILD WHO DIED IN CHILDBIRTH
SHORTLY AFTER.

HOWEVER, JACK AND JILL WERE
FREQUENTLY USED TO NAME ANY MAN
AND HIS PARTNER, HENCE TALES
LIKE JACK AND THE BEANSTALK.
EVEN SHAKESPEARE USES "JACK
WILL HAVE JILL" IN "LOVES LABOUR
LOST".
IT FIRST APPEARED IN PRINTED
FORM IN 1765 BUT IT IS PROBABLY
MUCH OLDER. SOME EVEN BELIEVE
THAT IT MAY HARK BACK TO NORSE
OR SAXON LEGENDS (PLAGUED WITH
JACKS).

THE VERSE ABOUT VINEGAR AND
BROWN PAPER SEEMS TO HAVE
BEEN ADDED AT A LATER DATE TO
SOFTEN THE BLOW.

HUMPTY DUMPTY
SAT ON THE WALL
HUMPTY DUMPTY
HAD A GREAT FALL
AND ALL THE KINGS HORSES
AND ALL THE KINGS MEN
COULDN'T PUT HUMPTY
TOGETHER AGAIN

HUMPTY DUMPTY FIRST APPEARED IN PRINT IN 1797.

HIS EGGY APPEARANCE WE OWE TO TENIEL, AND LEWIS CARROL MUCH LATER, WHERE HE APPEARS IN ALICE THROUGH THE LOOKING GLASS. TWO THEORIES HAVE HUMPTY DOWN AS A ROYALIST CANNON OR SIEGE WEAPON TUMBLED BY ROUNDHEAD SOLDIERS IN THE CIVIL WAR, WHICH WOULD EXPLAIN "ALL THE KINGS MEN". HE MAY HAVE BEEN THE DETHRONED AND EXECUTED KING CHARLES THE FIRST, OR CARDINAL WOLSEY, HENRY THE EIGHTTH'S RELIGIOUS ALLY. IT'S ALSO THOUGHT THAT HUMPTY DUMPTY MAY HAVE BEEN A GENERAL INSULT DIRECTED AT LARGE CLUMSY PEOPLE, WHICH COULD EXPLAIN BOTH THE NAME AND HIS EVOLUTION TO EGG-FORM. THERE WAS ALSO AN ALCOHOLIC DRINK NAMED "HUMPTY DUMPTY". IT'S PROBABLY FAIR TO GUESS THAT HUMPTY DUMPTY WASN'T A HIT IN ANY PALACE.

ROCK A BYE BABY
ON THE TREE TOP
WHEN THE WIND BLOWS
THE CRADLE WILL ROCK
WHEN THE BOW BREAKS
THE CRADLE WILL FALL
AND DOWN WILL COME BABY
CRADLE AND ALL

IT WAS FIRST PRINTED IN 1765 WITH HUSH A BYE, AND NOT ROCK A BYE.

WE DON'T EVEN KNOW WHERE THIS SONG IS FROM, AS IT MAY OR MAY NOT HAVE TRAVELLED BACK FROM AMERICA.

WAS IT INSPIRED BY NATIVE AMERICAN WOMEN SUSPENDING THEIR CHILDREN IN BIRCH BARK CRIBS THAT WOULD ROCK WITH THE WIND?

SOME THINK THE BABY IS THE POSSSIBLY ILLEGITIMATE AND UNWELCOME JAMES THE SECOND WHO TRIED TO REINSTATE CATHOLICISM AS STATE RELIGION AND HIMSELF AS DIVINE RULER.

SOME BELIEVE IT INSPIRED BY A DERBYSHIRE FAMILY WHO LIVED IN A HOLLOW YEW TREE. FINALLY IT MAY SIMPLY BE A SONG WITH A BUMP AT THE END, OR MAYBE THE DARK FANTASY OF AN EXASPERATED PARENT. WHATEVER THE ORIGINS, BABY IS ALONE, AND THEIR FATE UNCERTAIN.

A STRANGE LULLABY.

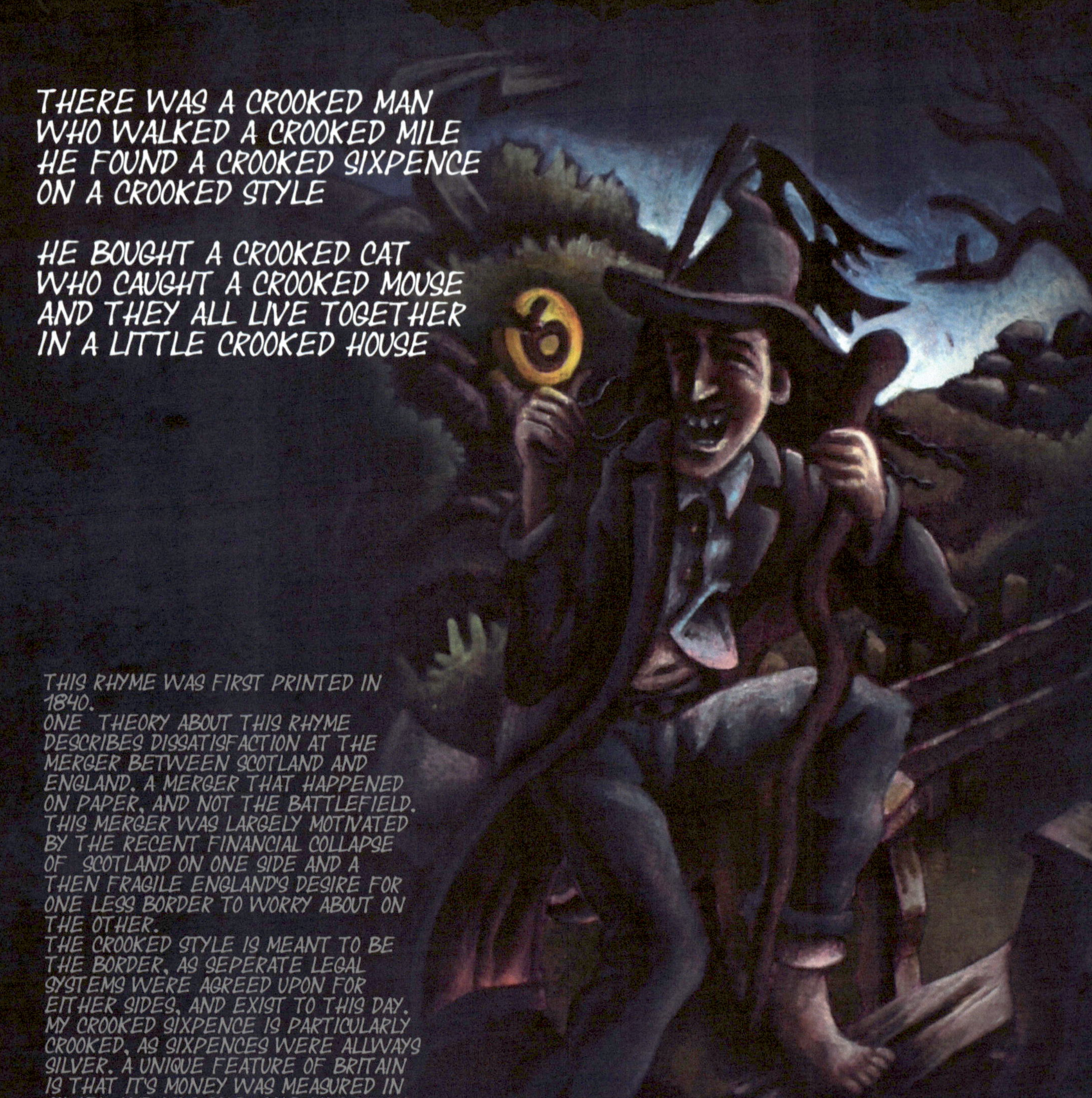
THERE WAS A CROOKED MAN
WHO WALKED A CROOKED MILE
HE FOUND A CROOKED SIXPENCE
ON A CROOKED STYLE

HE BOUGHT A CROOKED CAT
WHO CAUGHT A CROOKED MOUSE
AND THEY ALL LIVE TOGETHER
IN A LITTLE CROOKED HOUSE

THIS RHYME WAS FIRST PRINTED IN
1840.
ONE THEORY ABOUT THIS RHYME
DESCRIBES DISSATISFACTION AT THE
MERGER BETWEEN SCOTLAND AND
ENGLAND. A MERGER THAT HAPPENED
ON PAPER, AND NOT THE BATTLEFIELD.
THIS MERGER WAS LARGELY MOTIVATED
BY THE RECENT FINANCIAL COLLAPSE
OF SCOTLAND ON ONE SIDE AND A
THEN FRAGILE ENGLAND'S DESIRE FOR
ONE LESS BORDER TO WORRY ABOUT ON
THE OTHER.
THE CROOKED STYLE IS MEANT TO BE
THE BORDER, AS SEPERATE LEGAL
SYSTEMS WERE AGREED UPON FOR
EITHER SIDES, AND EXIST TO THIS DAY.
MY CROOKED SIXPENCE IS PARTICULARLY
CROOKED, AS SIXPENCES WERE ALLWAYS
SILVER. A UNIQUE FEATURE OF BRITAIN
IS THAT IT'S MONEY WAS MEASURED IN
SILVER AND NOT GOLD, GOLD NOT BEING
READILY AVAILABLE.

THIS OLD MAN HE PLAYED ONE
HE PLAYED NIK NAK ON MY THUMB
[CHORUS]
WITH A NIK NAK PADDYWACK
GIVE A DOG A BONE
THIS OLD MAN CAME ROLLING HOME

THIS OLD MAN HE PLAYED TWO
HE PLAYED NIK NAK ON MY SHOE
[CHORUS]
THIS OLD MAN HE PLAYED THREE
HE PLAYED NIK NAK ON MY KNEE
[CHORUS]
THIS OLD MAN HE PLAYED FOUR
HE PLAYED NIK NAK ON MY DOOR
[CHORUS]
THIS OLD MAN HE PLAYED FIVE
HE PLAYED NIK NAK ON MY HIVE
[CHORUS]
THIS OLD MAN HE PLAYED SIX
HE PLAYED NIK NAK ON MY STICKS
[CHORUS]
THIS OLD MAN HE PLAYED SEVEN
HE PLAYED NIK NAK UP IN HEAVEN
[CHORUS]
THIS OLD MAN HE PLAYED EIGHT
HE PLAYED NIK NAK ON MY GATE
[CHORUS]
THIS OLD MAN HE PLAYED NINE
HE PLAYED NIK NAK ON MY SPINE
[CHORUS]
THIS OLD MAN HE PLAYED TEN
HE PLAYED NIK NAK ONCE AGAIN
[CHORUS]

THIS LATE COMER FIRST APPEARED 1906
IN PRINT, BUT MOST SCHOLARS AGREE
THAT IT'S OLDER.
THE OLD MAN MAY BE A TINKER, OR A
DISPLACED IRISHMAN DURING OR AFTER
THE GREAT POTATO FAMINE IN THE
NINETEETH CENTURY WHERE MILLIONS
RELOCATED AND MILLIONS MORE DIED
OF STARVATION, BUT THE USE OF
LANGUAGE, BOTH NUMBER RHYMES AND
WORDS THAT MAY OR MAY NOT BE JUST
SOUNDS MAKE IT HARD TO PROBE.
OLD MEN HAVE A ROUGH TIME IN
NURSERY RHYMES.

HALF A POIUND OF TUPPENNY RICE
HALF A POUND OF TREACLE
THAT'S THE WAY THE MONEY GOES
POP GOES THE WEASEL

EVERY NIGHT WHEN I GO OUT
THE MONKEY'S ON THE TABLE
TAKE A STICK AND KNOCK IT OFF
POP GOES THE WEASEL

UP AND DOWN THE CITY ROAD
IN AND OUT THE EAGLE
THATS THE WAY THE MONEY GOES
POP GOES THE WEASEL

UNLIKE MANY RHYMES WHICH POSSIBLY
GAINED OR BORROWED THE TUNE AT A
LATER DATE, POP GOES THE
WEASEL MAY HAVE BEGUN AS A DANCE,
AS THAT IS HOW IT FIRST APPEARS IN
PRINT, IN 1853, ACCOMPANIED ONLY BY
ITS TITLE AND FOURTH LINE.

THE FIRST VERSE IS PRETTY MUCH
UNIVERSAL BUT THE SECOND AND THIRD
HERE ARE JUST COMMONLY ADDED
VERSES. THERE ARE MANY OTHER
VERSES KNOWN, AND OFTEN THEY ARE
WILDLY DIFFERENT.

THERE ARE MANY GUESSES AS TO WHAT
THE WEASEL THEMSELF MIGHT BE:
A WEAVING TOOL OF THE SAME NAME,
COCKNEY SLANG FOR THE THROAT, A FUR
COAT, OR EVEN A WEASEL. MENTION
OF CITY, AND WHAT MANY BELIEVE TO
BE THE EAGLE PUB IN LONDON MAKES
A SHY ANIMAL'S APPEARANCE IN THIS
RHYME FAIRLY SURREAL THOUGH.

THIS SONG FREQUENTLY FEATURES ON
JACK IN THE BOX TOYS.

BAA BAA BLACK SHEEP
HAVE YOU ANY WOOL
YES SIR, YES SIR,
THREE BAGS FULL
ONES FOR THE MASTER
ONES FOR THE DAME
AND ONES FOR THE LITTLE BOY
WHO LIVES DOWN THE LANE

BAA BAA BLACK SHEEP CAN BE TRACED BACK TO 1736. THE MELODY IS BORROWED AGAIN FROM "AH VOIS DIRAIS JE MAMAN".

IN SOME EARLY VERSIONS THE SHEEP DOLED OUT TWO SACKS TO THE MASTER, AND "NONE FOR THE LITTLE BOY WHO WEEPS DOWN THE LANE", MOCKING THE GREED OF THE WEALTHY.

THERE WAS CONTROVERSY OVER THE BLACKNESS OF THE SHEEP, AND MANY FELT THAT IT MAY HAVE RACIST CONNOTATIONS, BUT MOST HISTORIANS AGREE THAT THE BLACK SHEEP, GROVELLING OR NOT, IS A SYMBOL OF VALUE AND WEALTH, AS OPPOSED TO AN OSTRACISED UNDERCLASS. (SHEEP MIGHT DISAGREE)

BLACK WOOL WAS VALUED, AS IT MADE DARK CLOTHES WITH LESS EFFORT.

"YES SIR, THREE BAGS FULL SIR" HAS ENTERED THE COLLECTIVE CONSCIOUSNESS AS A PHRASE DENOTING UNNECCESARY SUBSERVIANCE, OR INDEED A DEMAND FOR IT. WHICH GIVES AN UNFORTUNATE CONNECTION WITH RACIAL STEREOTYPES, EVEN THOUGH IT USUALLY DENOTED TENSIONS OF CLASS AND AUTHORITY.

SAD TO THINK THAT THE VOICE OF ONE MISTREATED GROUP CAN BE TURNED AGAINST ANOTHER.

RUB A DUB DUB
THREE MEN IN THE TUB
WHO DO YOU THINK THEY'LL BE
THE BUTCHER, THE BAKER
THE CANDLESTICK MAKER
AND ALL OF THEM OUT TO SEA

THESE THREE UNFORTUNATE MEN
CAN BE TRACED ALL THE WAY BACK
TO THE FOURTEENTH CENTURY, BUT
IT APPEARS THAT A LITTLE SPRING
CLEANING HAS ALREADY HAPPENED
HERE AS ORIGINALLY THERE WERE
THREE MAIDS IN THE TUB, OUR DODGY
TRIO ACTING AS NAUGHTY BYSTANDERS.

THE "TUB" IS BELIEVED TO BE A
FAIRGROUND PEEP SHOW. SOMEHOW
OVER THE YEARS THE MAIDS
DISAPPEARED AND THE CARNIVAL WITH
THEM, LEAVING THESE POOR SOULS OUT
TO SEA WITH A RATHER DESPERATE
MAKESHIFT BOAT. IT CONJURES IN
THE MIND AN ALMOST FAUST LIKE
STORY OF TEMPTATION FOLLOWED BY
DAMNATION.

MANY BELIEVE THAT THE CHOICE OF
BUTCHER BAKER AND CANDLESTICK
MAKER WAS MOCKING THE MORALITY OF
A SUPPOSEDLY "RESPECTABLE" MIDDLE
CLASSES.

10 GREEN BOTTLES
HANGING ON THE WALL
10 GREEN BOTTLES
HANGING ON THE WALL
AND IF ONE GREEN BOTTLE
SHOULD ACCIDENTALLY FALL
THERE'LL BE 9 GREEN BOTTLES
HANGING ON THE WALL

9 GREEN BOTTLES....
(AND SO ON, UNTIL "NO GREEN
BOTTLES")

HANGING?

BOTTLES?

ACCORDING TO ONE POPULAR THEORY
GREEN BOTTLES WAS ONE OF THE
LESS AFFECTIONATE TERMS FOR THE
NEWLY FORMED "BOBBIES" OR POLICE
FORCE, ESTABLISHED BY ROBERT
PEEL IN 1822.

THE IDEA OF A DEDICATED POLICE
FORCE ALMOST UNDOUBTEDLY
WAS GROUNDED IN THE BEST OF
INTENTIONS, REPLACING THE
MONARCHY BIASED ARMY AND THE
WAYWARD MOB, OR "POSSES" TO
PROVIDE JUSTICE FOR ALL, BUT IT
WAS NOT LONG BEFORE AT LEAST
SOME PEOPLE BEGAN TO ACTIVELY
DISTRUST AND DISLIKE THEM.

NATURALLY THE POLICE WERE
ASSOCIATED WITH THE THEN COMMON
PLACE HANGMAN'S ROPE, AND ALSO
NATURALLY MANY, PARTICULARLY THE
GENUINELY CRIMINAL ELEMENT,
SOMETIMES LIKED TO PICTURE THE
FAVOUR RETURNED.

RING A RING OF ROSES
A POCKET FULL OF ROSES
ATISHOO
ATISHOO
WE ALL FALL DOWN

EARLIEST PRINTS OF THIS RHYME ARE
IN THE EARLY NINETEENTH CENTURY,
BUT IT IS MENTIONED IN THE
EIGHTEENTH CENTURY AT LEAST, AND
COULD BE MUCH OLDER.

IT IS COMMONLY BELIEVED THAT IT
REFERENCES THE PLAGUE OR BLACK
DEATH, BUT IT'S TRUE ORIGINS ARE
UNCERTAIN, AND MANY VERSIONS WITH
DIFFERENT WORDING EXIST, SOME
OF WHICH HAVE NO CONNECTION TO
PLAGUE AT ALL.

STRIKINGLY SIMILAR RHYMES ARE
ALSO FOUND IN EASTERN EUROPE.
SURPRISINGLY, IT'S TRUE ORIGINS MAY
BE IN OUR PAGAN PAST. THE RING
DANCE RESEMBLING THE DANCE OF
THE MAY POLE. MANY OF THE LESS
KNOWN VARIANTS FEATURE SUCH
THINGS AS EGGS AND COWS IN PLACE
OF POSIES AND SNEEZES.

THE COMMON HABIT OF USING
THE TUNE WITH ALTERED WORDS
TO CELEBRATE THE FEARS,
WEAKNESSES AND INFIRMITIES OF
SOME UNFORTUNATE SOUL MAY BE THE
DARKEST SIDE OF THIS OLD RHYME.

HEY DIDDLE DIDDLE
THE CAT AND THE FIDDLE
THE COW JUMPED
OVER THE MOON
THE LITTLE DOG LAUGHED
TO SEE FUN
AND THE DISH RAN AWAY
WITH THE SPOON

THIS SURREAL AND YET CHEERFUL
NONSENSE RHYME MAY BE ONE
OF THE OLDEST IN THIS BOOK, AND
HAS A GUESSED AGE OF ANYTHING
BETWEEN ABOUT FIVE HUNDRED AND
A THOUSAND YEARS.

THAT WOULD MAKE IT OLDER THAN
THE LANGUAGE IT'S WRITTEN IN,
WOW!

THE CAT AND FIDDLE MOTIF APPEARS
IN NAMES OF PUBS, AND HAS
REFERENCES IN VARIOUS MEDIEVAL
TEXTS AND IMAGES, AS DOES THE
PHRASE "HEY DIDDLE DIDDLE".

THEORIES ABOUND AS TO IT'S
MEANING, INCLUDING VARIOUS KINGS
AND QUEENS , HISTORICAL EVENTS,
GREEK AND EGYPTIAN MYTHOLOGY TO
NAME JUST SOME.

IT MAY JUST BE A VERY EARLY
CELEBRATION OF FANTASY, FOLLY,
AND CHAOS.

THE "FUN" THAT THE DOG LAUGHS AT
IS SOMETIMES REPLACED BY "SPORT"
OR "CRAFT".

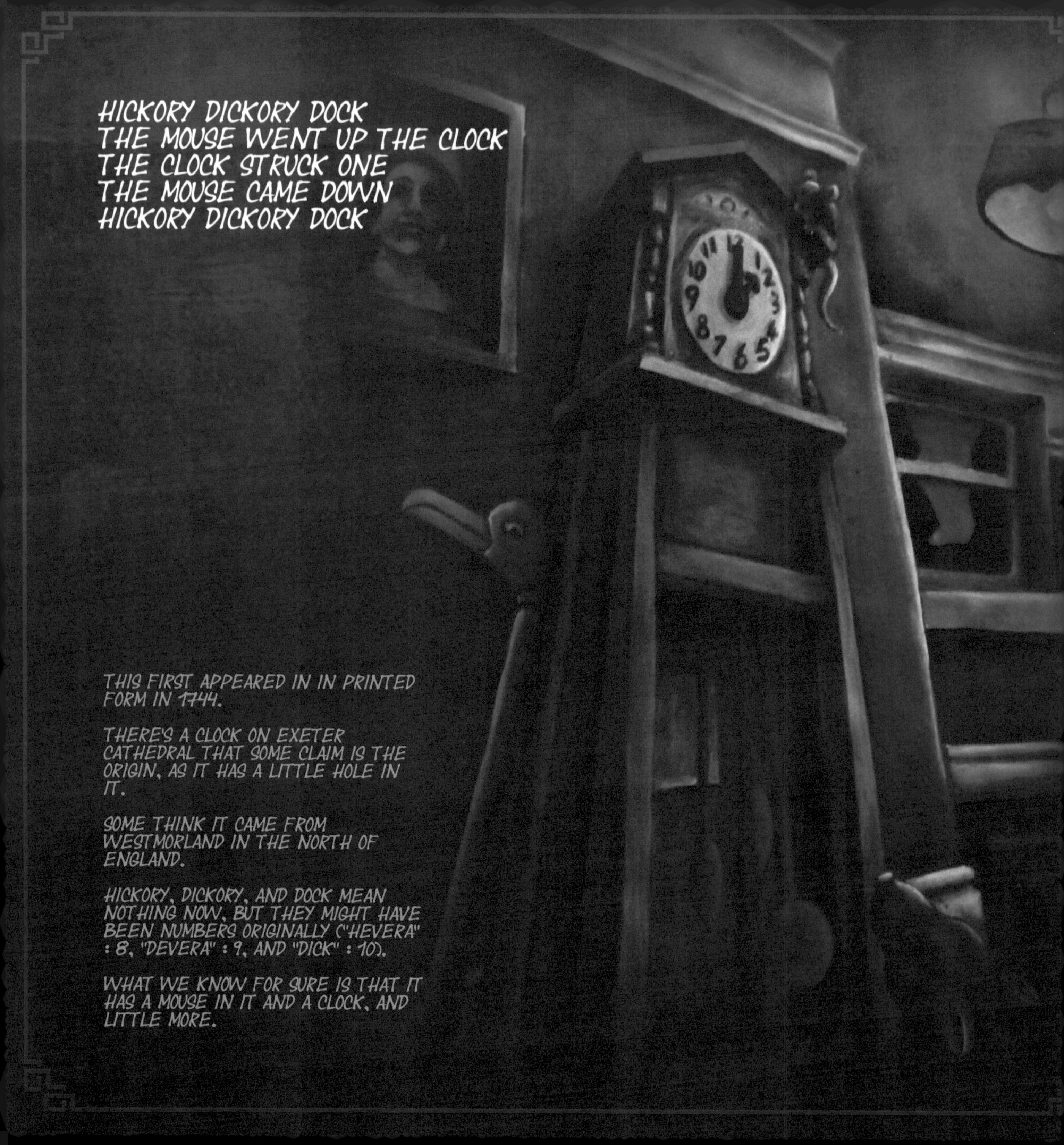

HICKORY DICKORY DOCK
THE MOUSE WENT UP THE CLOCK
THE CLOCK STRUCK ONE
THE MOUSE CAME DOWN
HICKORY DICKORY DOCK

THIS FIRST APPEARED IN IN PRINTED FORM IN 1744.

THERE'S A CLOCK ON EXETER CATHEDRAL THAT SOME CLAIM IS THE ORIGIN, AS IT HAS A LITTLE HOLE IN IT.

SOME THINK IT CAME FROM WESTMORLAND IN THE NORTH OF ENGLAND.

HICKORY, DICKORY, AND DOCK MEAN NOTHING NOW, BUT THEY MIGHT HAVE BEEN NUMBERS ORIGINALLY ("HEVERA" : 8, "DEVERA" : 9, AND "DICK" : 10).

WHAT WE KNOW FOR SURE IS THAT IT HAS A MOUSE IN IT AND A CLOCK, AND LITTLE MORE.

INCY WINCY SPIDER
CLIMBED UP THE SPOUT
DOWN CAME THE RAIN
AND WASHED THE SPIDER OUT
OUT CAME THE SUN
DRIED UP THE RAIN
AND INCY WINCY SPIDER
CLIMBED BACK UP AGAIN

INCY WINCY HAS AN ALIAS. HE IS ALSO FREQUENTLY CALLED "ITSY BITSY", PARTICULARLY IN AMERICA.

IT'S EARLIEST PRINT WAS IN 1910 IN AN AMERICAN BOY SCOUT BOOK, SO IT'S ORIGINS MAY BE IN AMERICA. THE SPOUT MAY BE A SPOUT FROM A KETTLE OR TEAPOT, BUT IS MOST LIKELY THE SPOUT OF A DRAIN.

SPIDERS PLAY A STRANGE ROLE IN CULTURE, FEATURING AS THE PERSEVERING UNDERDOG, THE MESSENGER OF GODS, AND THE HORRID THING WITH DANGLY LEGS.

A LEGENDARY ENCOUNTER WITH A SPIDER INSPIRES ROBERT THE BRUCE TO CONTINUE HIS REBELLION IN SCOTLAND, AND ONE SPIDER EVEN PROTECTS THE PROPHET MOHAMED WHILST HE HIDES IN A CAVE.

SO THE RHYME MAY BE PARABLE OF INSPIRATION OR MAYBE A WAY TO FREAK EACH OTHER OUT.

FIRST PRINT HAS HIM CALLED "BLOODY BLOODY SPIDER", MAYBE THERE'S A CLUE IN THAT.

BROTHER JOHN
BROTHER JOHN
ARE YOU AWAKE
ARE YOU AWAKE
MORNING BELLS ARE RINGING
MORNING BELLS ARE RINGING
DING DANG DONG
DING DANG DONG

THIS SONG IS FRENCH BUT ALSO WELL
KNOWN IN THE UK NOW. IT'S ORIGINAL
WORDS ARE AS FOLLOWS:

FRERE JAQUES
FRERE JAQUES
DORMEZ VOUS
DORMEZ VOUS
SOMMEIL A MATINE
SOMMEIL A MATINE
DING DANG DONG
DING DANG DONG

THE FRIAR IS ASLEEP, AND IT'S
LUNCHTIME IN THE FRENCH VERSION,
AND THE CLOSEST NAME TO HIS IS JACK
OR JAMES, BUT OTHER THAN THAT IT IS
LARGELY UNCHANGED.

IT'S FIRST PRINTED MENTION IS DATED
1780. SOME BELIEVE IT A TAUNT AIMED
AT DOMINICAN PRIESTS ,PROTESTANTS OR
JEWS.

I GUESS THAT IN A STRANGE WAY IT'S
GOOD TO KNOW THAT GOOSEY WASN'T THE
ONLY BIGGOT AT THE TABLE.

CONVERSELY, IT MAY DESCRIBE A PRIEST
FAMED BUT NOT ENTIRELY ADMIRED FOR
HIS SURGICAL PURSUITS.

LIKE RING OF ROSES, THIS SONG HAD
VARIANTS ALL OVER EUROPE LONG BEFORE
TELEVISION OR THE WEB.

GANDER GANDER GAGAGA
MUM'S A WITCH A RAGANA
AND THIS WITCH SHE BAKED A
CAKE
BUT SHE WILL NEVER LET YOU
TAKE
GANDER GANDER TURN AROUND
IN YOUR BOOTS A FROG YOU FOUND
GANDER GANDER TURN AROUND
IN YOUR BOOTS A FROG YOU FOUND

NOW IT'S MY TURN TO "GET CREATIVE"..
THIS WAS FIRSTLY TRANSLATED FROM LITHUANIAN
BY THE ONE WHO TOLD IT TO ME, BUT THEN I MADE
IT'S RHYME AND PATTERN FIT.

GANDRAI, GANDRAI, GAGAGA
TAVO MOČIA RAGANA
TAU BANDELe IšKEPė,
KAD IR KEPė NEDAVė
GANDRAI, GANDRAI APSUK RATa,
GAUSI VARLe i čIABATa čIABATa

GANDRAI IS "STORK", AND NOT GANDER BUT A BIT
OF DIGGING STRETCHES GANDRAI AND GANDER TO
THE SAME PROTO INDO EUROPEAN ROOT WORD,
GANDRA, MEANING GOOSE. THIS IS AN INTERESTING
CONNECTION AS IT ASSOCIATES THE STORK, GOOSE
AND GANNET (ANOTHER LONG NECKED AQUATIC BIRD.

NOTABLY THE GOOSE, THE STORK, AND OTHER
SIMILAR BIRDS ARE LINKED WITH THE MOTHER, IN
PARALLEL TO THE IBIS WITH ISIS AND THE HERON
WITH THE NORSE FRIGGA.

LITHUANIAN HISTORIANS NOTE THAT RELIGIOUS
PERSECUTION WAS PARTICULARLY SOFT IN LITHUANIA
AND MANY MORE PAGAN REMNANTS PERSIST,
PARTICULARLY CELTIC PAGAN.

TOLERANCE THERE MAY HAVE PRESERVED WHAT
REMOTENESS PRESERVED IN THE UK.

STRANGE TO HAVE SUCH A CULTURAL NEIGHBOUR SO
DISTANT.

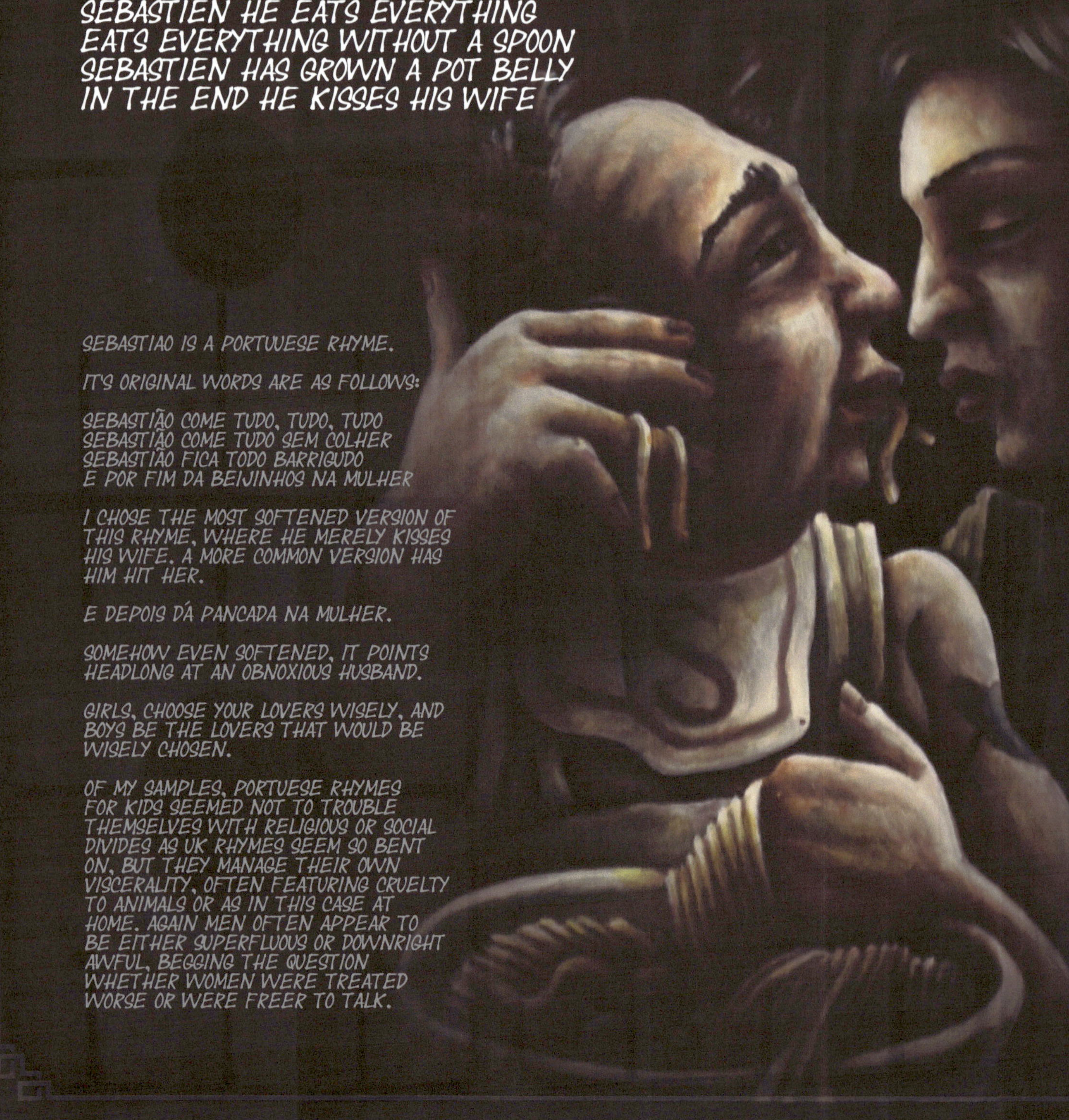

SEBASTIEN HE EATS EVERYTHING
EATS EVERYTHING WITHOUT A SPOON
SEBASTIEN HAS GROWN A POT BELLY
IN THE END HE KISSES HIS WIFE

SEBASTIAO IS A PORTUUESE RHYME.

IT'S ORIGINAL WORDS ARE AS FOLLOWS:

SEBASTIÃO COME TUDO, TUDO, TUDO
SEBASTIÃO COME TUDO SEM COLHER
SEBASTIÃO FICA TODO BARRIGUDO
E POR FIM DA BEIJINHOS NA MULHER

I CHOSE THE MOST SOFTENED VERSION OF
THIS RHYME, WHERE HE MERELY KISSES
HIS WIFE. A MORE COMMON VERSION HAS
HIM HIT HER.

E DEPOIS DÁ PANCADA NA MULHER.

SOMEHOW EVEN SOFTENED, IT POINTS
HEADLONG AT AN OBNOXIOUS HUSBAND.

GIRLS, CHOOSE YOUR LOVERS WISELY, AND
BOYS BE THE LOVERS THAT WOULD BE
WISELY CHOSEN.

OF MY SAMPLES, PORTUESE RHYMES
FOR KIDS SEEMED NOT TO TROUBLE
THEMSELVES WITH RELIGIOUS OR SOCIAL
DIVIDES AS UK RHYMES SEEM SO BENT
ON, BUT THEY MANAGE THEIR OWN
VISCERALITY, OFTEN FEATURING CRUELTY
TO ANIMALS OR AS IN THIS CASE AT
HOME. AGAIN MEN OFTEN APPEAR TO
BE EITHER SUPERFLUOUS OR DOWNRIGHT
AWFUL, BEGGING THE QUESTION
WHETHER WOMEN WERE TREATED
WORSE OR WERE FREER TO TALK.

WHEN THE MOON WAS BORN
AND GREW IN THE BEYOND
THE NIGHT IT FOLLOWED ON HIGH.
SO SLEEP, MY CHILD
SO SLEEP AND DREAM
LET THE MOON RISE UP IN THE SKY

THE RATTLE IT FELL
AND LOST IT'S THREADS
IT'S EYES WILL CLOSE SOFTLY SOON
AS NOTHING COULD STOP
THE BABY SLEEPS WELL.
NEITHER FEAR WILL COME NOR ANYONE

YOU'LL SEE, MY LOVE.
HOW SWEET IT IS TO DREAM
GOD WILL GIVE YOU SO WELL
MY ANGEL DO OH
BECAUSE I SEE YOU
ONLY ANGELS WILL SEE THE MOON SMILE.

THIS IS A TRANSLATION OF A PORTUGUESE LULLABY.

IT'S TRUE WORDS ARE BELOW:

A LUA NASCEU E CRESCEU NO ALÉM
A NOITE CHEGOU TAMBÉM
VAI DORMIR MEU BEBÉ
VAI DORMIR E SONHAR
DEIXA A LUA CRESCER LÁ NO AR

A ROCA POISOU E LARGOU SEM CHORAR
OS OLHOS VAI JÁ FECHAR
NADA PODE IMPEDIR
QUE O BEBÉ DURMA BEM
NEM PAPÃO HÁ-DE VIR
NEM NINGUÉM

TU VERÁS MEU AMOR
COMO É BOM SONHOS TER
DEUS TE DÊ O MELHOR QUE HOUVER
ANJO MEU FAZ Ó Ó
PORQUE EU VELO POR TI
SÓ AOS ANJOS A LUA SORRI.

IT'S SOMEHOW A BIT OVER-SOPHISTICATED FOR
THIS BOOK AT A GUESS, BUT MAKES A COMFORTING
CONCLUSION.

GRATITUDE

THANK YOU FOR BUYING THIS BOOK.

IT IS DEDICATED TO MY SON JETHRO WHO HAS PLAYED VERSIONS OF THESE RHYMES WAY TOO OFTEN ON THE COMPUTER.

IF YOU'VE GOT THE BUG DON'T TRUST ME, GO FIND OUT. THERE'S A LOT OF INTERESTING FACTS THAT WOULDN'T FIT HERE, AND ALOT OF INTERESTING FICTIONS TOO.

ALL OF THE SONGS CAME EITHER FROM MY CHILDHOOD OR FROM THE CHILDHOOD OF PEOPLE I KNOW. THAT MAKES THEM AUTHENTIC AT LEAST TO ONE TIME.

MOST OF THE EXTRA RESEARCH CAME FROM THE WEB.

WIKIPEDIA.ORG
ENTYMONLINE.ORG
RHYMES.ORG.UK
YOUTUBE.COM
SACREDTEXTS.ORG

OTHER REFERENNCE POINTS WERE A BIT OF HISTORY, AND A LOVE OF MYTHOLOGY BUT I'VE TRIED TO KEEP IMPARTIAL.

THANKS TO INES AND KRISTINA FOR SHARING PORTUGUESE AND LITHUANIAN NURSERY RHYMES.

THANKS TO MY FAMILY FOR... WELL... COPING.

THANKS TO MY FRIENDS FOR LENDING AN EAR.

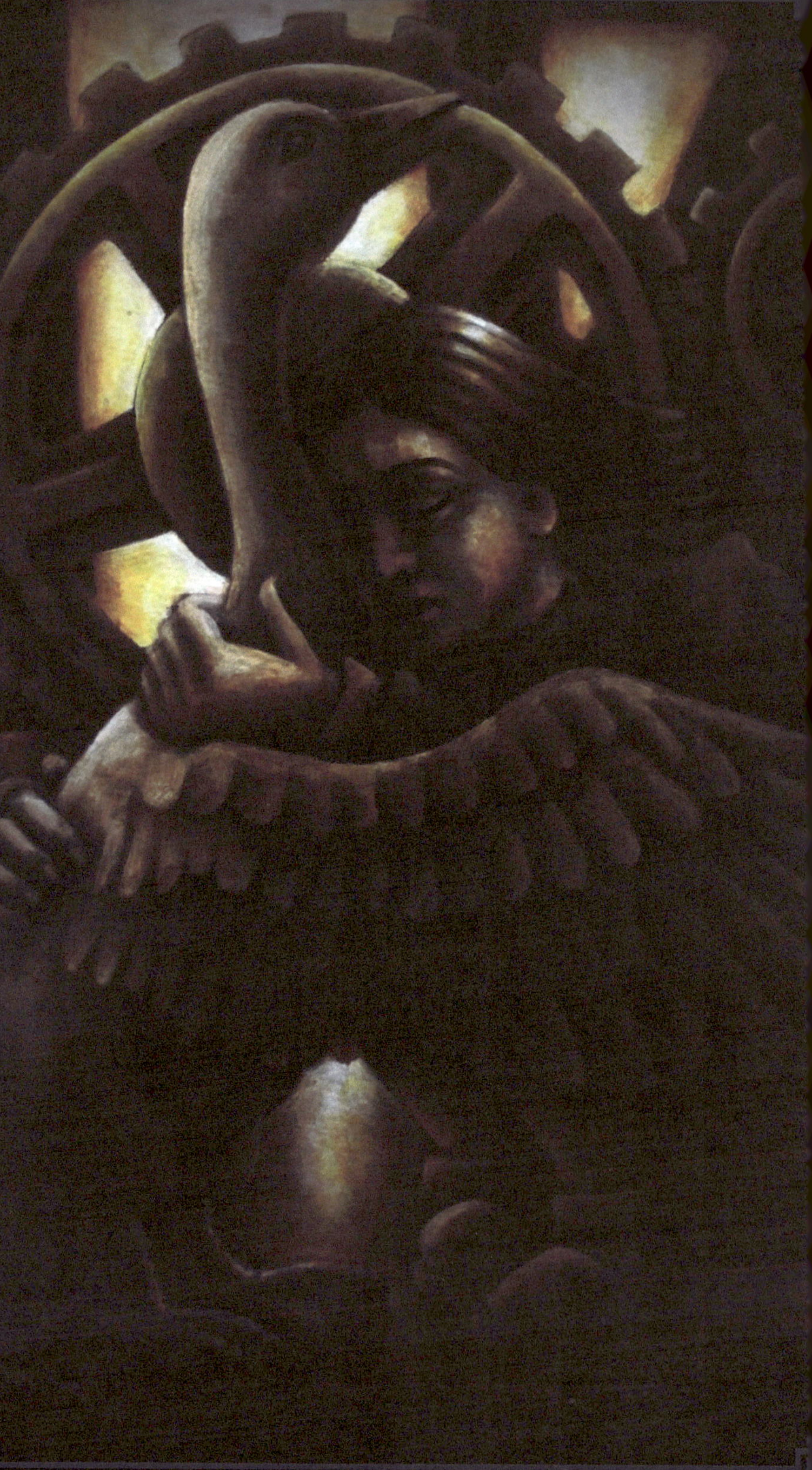